My
TRUTH

Copyright © 2017 by Marie P. Cetoute—Tides Center for Growth, LLC

Website: www.mariecetoute.com

ISBN: 0-9984675-0-2
ISBN-13: 978-0-9984-6750-4

Printed in the United States of America

10 9 8 7 6 5 4 3 2 1

First Edition: 2017

Kimia Alipanah

Introduction

How would you like to learn ways to master greater control over your life? It is possible by first mastering command of your thoughts, words and emotions. All three influence how we experience life. In addition, many studies confirm the healing powers of processing life events and emotional topics through writing.

The purpose of this journal is to serve as a resource to help you gain greater control managing your thoughts, words and emotions. It is possible through acknowledging yourself and giving a voice to all that is within you, using positive practices to foster a growth mindset and having an outlet to calm your mind. As a result, you will harness natural powers to support being your best self.

In this journal, you do not have to worry about punctuation, proper grammar, or neatness. Most importantly, use the blank pages as a judgment-free space to candidly explore all areas of your life as you express your deepest thoughts and emotions. Also, you are encouraged to emphasize your positive attributes and life circumstances as well as manage your negative self-talk.

How to manage negative self-talk?

To affirm is to acknowledge and accept something to be true. Some of the ways we affirm is by verbalizing statements, using visualization or mentally repeating thoughts we believe – the good or negative. It is often easy to affirm berating thoughts about ourselves or life. Consequently, we fall into the trap of believing and repeating a significant amount of negative self-talk. Then, we become what we believe and affirmed.

You can govern the negative self-talk by repeating an "I am" affirmation that is positively worded, builds you up and strengthens you toward becoming who you want to be. It is very important to remain mindful of the words that follow your "I am" since you become and live your words. Your "I am" is a declaration. It is best not to focus on who you are not or what seem impossible.

Reference: Baikie, K.A., Wilhelm, K. (2005). Emotional and physical health benefits of expressive writing. *BJPsych Advances in Psychiatric Treatment, 11*(5), 338-346.

For instance, mindlessly affirming "I am lazy" creates experiences where you limit yourself. Instead, choosing to affirm statements like "I am a go-getter" or "I am hard-working" create experiences that attract it as your reality. At first you may not believe the affirmation but it is attainable with continuous practice.

What are key components of a positive affirmation?

- Present tense wording – propels it to quickly become a reality
- Focuses on positives and potential – words like "can" and "possible"
- Create positive internal experiences – feeling hopeful and strong

What are not components of a positive affirmation?

- Negative wording and forecasts doom – repels the desired experience
- Focuses on limits or inabilities – words like "can't" or "never"
- Create negative internal experiences – feeling hopeless and powerless

Your aim is not to completely erase the natural experiencing of negative thoughts. If they appear, it is important to deliberately refocus and rehearse positive statements instead. By doing so, you are not giving negative thoughts your attention and time thereby weakening their influence. With time and consistent practice, the negative thoughts will be infrequent and easily redirected. Keep in mind not to berate yourself for the number of times you refocus your thoughts. Subsequently, you will gain greater control of your life.

How will this journal help?

In addition to the writing space provided, this journal offers an opportunity to practice refocusing negative self-talk through using positive "I am" affirmations. Every page provides space for creating a personal "I am" affirmation. There are also guided "I am" affirmations that offer examples you can rehearse—with a full list in the last few pages of the journal. Feel free to highlight from the list what resonates with you, and use them when the negative thoughts are overwhelming.

Now, take the time to discover all that is within you, connect with your inner guide and affirm the life you desire.

My Empowering Affirmation:
I am _____

Guided Affirmation: **I am focusing my mind on positive thoughts and images.**

My Empowering Affirmation:
I am _____

Guided Affirmation: **I am giving my best and providing value to others.**

My Empowering Affirmation:
I am _____

Guided Affirmation: **I am worthy.**

My Empowering Affirmation:
I am _____

Guided Affirmation: **I am giving my best and providing value to others.**

My Empowering Affirmation:
I am _____

Guided Affirmation: **I am creating life goals that are inspiring and realistic.**

My Empowering Affirmation:
I am _____

Guided Affirmation: **I am giving my best and providing value to others.**

My Empowering Affirmation:
I am _____

Guided Affirmation: **I am joyful.**

My Empowering Affirmation:
I am _____

Guided Affirmation: **I am giving my best and providing value to others.**

My Empowering Affirmation:
I am _____

Guided Affirmation: **I am composed, even during moments of trouble.**

My Empowering Affirmation:
I am _____

Guided Affirmation: **I am giving my best and providing value to others.**

My Empowering Affirmation:
I am _____

Guided Affirmation: **I am deserving.**

My Empowering Affirmation:
I am _____

Guided Affirmation: **I am giving my best and providing value to others.**

My Empowering Affirmation:
I am _____

Guided Affirmation: **I am goal-oriented and taking action.**

My Empowering Affirmation:
I am _____

Guided Affirmation: **I am giving my best and providing value to others.**

My Empowering Affirmation:
I am _____

Guided Affirmation: **I am calm and feeling peaceful.**

My Empowering Affirmation:
I am _____

Guided Affirmation: **I am giving my best and providing value to others.**

My Empowering Affirmation:
I am _____

Guided Affirmation: **I am releasing fear and feeling bold.**

My Empowering Affirmation:
I am _____

Guided Affirmation: **I am giving my best and providing value to others.**

My Empowering Affirmation:
I am _____

Guided Affirmation: **I am thinking clearly and optimistically.**

My Empowering Affirmation:
I am _____

Guided Affirmation: **I am giving my best and providing value to others.**

My Empowering Affirmation:
I am _____

Guided Affirmation: **I am unstoppable.**

My Empowering Affirmation:
I am _____

Guided Affirmation: **I am giving my best and providing value to others.**

My Empowering Affirmation:
I am _____

Guided Affirmation: **I am focused, and actively creating my dreams.**

My Empowering Affirmation:
I am _____

Guided Affirmation: **I am giving my best and providing value to others.**

My Empowering Affirmation:
I am _____

Guided Affirmation: **I am overcoming challenges.**

My Empowering Affirmation:
I am _____

Guided Affirmation: **I am giving my best and providing value to others.**

My Empowering Affirmation:
I am _____

Guided Affirmation: **I am deserving of feeling joy and peace.**

My Empowering Affirmation:
I am _____

Guided Affirmation: **I am giving my best and providing value to others.**

My Empowering Affirmation:
I am _____

Guided Affirmation: **I am confident and powerful.**

My Empowering Affirmation:
I am _____

Guided Affirmation: **I am giving my best and providing value to others.**

My Empowering Affirmation:
I am _____

Guided Affirmation: **I am imaginative.**

My Empowering Affirmation:
I am _____

Guided Affirmation: **I am giving my best and providing value to others.**

My Empowering Affirmation:
I am _____

Guided Affirmation: **I am releasing disappointment and feeling grateful.**

My Empowering Affirmation:
I am _____

Guided Affirmation: **I am giving my best and providing value to others.**

My Empowering Affirmation:
I am _____

Guided Affirmation: **I am confidently repeating powerful thoughts.**

My Empowering Affirmation:
I am _____

Guided Affirmation: **I am giving my best and providing value to others.**

My Empowering Affirmation:
I am _____

Guided Affirmation: **I am grateful.**

My Empowering Affirmation:
I am _____

Guided Affirmation: **I am giving my best and providing value to others.**

My Empowering Affirmation:
I am _____

Guided Affirmation: **I am designing and living a joyful life.**

My Empowering Affirmation:
I am _____

Guided Affirmation: **I am giving my best and providing value to others.**

My Empowering Affirmation:
I am _____

Guided Affirmation: **I am successfully managing my problems.**

My Empowering Affirmation:
I am _____

Guided Affirmation: **I am giving my best and providing value to others.**

My Empowering Affirmation:
I am _____

Guided Affirmation: **I am good enough.**

My Empowering Affirmation:
I am _____

Guided Affirmation: **I am giving my best and providing value to others.**

My Empowering Affirmation:
I am _____

Guided Affirmation: **I am intelligent and gifted.**

My Empowering Affirmation:
I am _____

Guided Affirmation: **I am giving my best and providing value to others.**

My Empowering Affirmation:
I am _____

Guided Affirmation: **I am self-compassionate.**

My Empowering Affirmation:
I am _____

Guided Affirmation: **I am giving my best and providing value to others.**

My Empowering Affirmation:
I am _____

Guided Affirmation: **I am releasing doubt and feeling confident.**

My Empowering Affirmation:
I am _____

Guided Affirmation: **I am giving my best and providing value to others.**

My Empowering Affirmation:
I am _____

Guided Affirmation: **I am repeating positive and affirming thoughts.**

My Empowering Affirmation:
I am _____

Guided Affirmation: **I am giving my best and providing value to others.**

My Empowering Affirmation:
I am _____

Guided Affirmation: **I am passionate.**

My Empowering Affirmation:
I am _____

Guided Affirmation: **I am giving my best and providing value to others.**

My Empowering Affirmation:
I am _____

Guided Affirmation: **I am creating a happy and fulfilling life.**

My Empowering Affirmation:
I am _____

Guided Affirmation: **I am giving my best and providing value to others.**

My Empowering Affirmation:
I am _____

Guided Affirmation: **I am focused and disciplined.**

My Empowering Affirmation:
I am _____

Guided Affirmation: **I am giving my best and providing value to others.**

My Empowering Affirmation:
I am _____

Guided Affirmation: **I am living a purposeful life.**

My Empowering Affirmation:
I am _____

Guided Affirmation: **I am giving my best and providing value to others.**

My Empowering Affirmation:
I am _____

Guided Affirmation: **I am releasing sorrow and feeling hopeful.**

My Empowering Affirmation:
I am _____

Guided Affirmation: **I am giving my best and providing value to others.**

My Empowering Affirmation:
I am _____

Guided Affirmation: **I am nurturing an abundance mindset.**

My Empowering Affirmation:
I am _____

Guided Affirmation: **I am giving my best and providing value to others.**

My Empowering Affirmation:
I am _____

Guided Affirmation: **I am dependable.**

My Empowering Affirmation:
I am _____

Guided Affirmation: **I am giving my best and providing value to others.**

My Empowering Affirmation:
I am _____

Guided Affirmation: **I am creating my happiness.**

My Empowering Affirmation:
I am _____

Guided Affirmation: **I am giving my best and providing value to others.**

My Empowering Affirmation:
I am _____

Guided Affirmation: **I am manifesting my dreams.**

My Empowering Affirmation:
I am _____

Guided Affirmation: **I am giving my best and providing value to others.**

My Empowering Affirmation:
I am _____

Guided Affirmation: **I am worthy of all good things that come my way.**

My Empowering Affirmation:
I am _____

Guided Affirmation: **I am giving my best and providing value to others.**

My Empowering Affirmation:
I am _____

Guided Affirmation: **I am unique and magnificent.**

My Empowering Affirmation:
I am _____

Guided Affirmation: **I am giving my best and providing value to others.**

My Empowering Affirmation:
I am _____

Guided Affirmation: **I am intentional in all areas of my life.**

My Empowering Affirmation:
I am _____

Guided Affirmation: **I am giving my best and providing value to others.**

My Empowering Affirmation:
I am _____

Guided Affirmation: **I am releasing envy and feeling love.**

My Empowering Affirmation:
I am _____

Guided Affirmation: **I am giving my best and providing value to others.**

My Empowering Affirmation:
I am _____

Guided Affirmation: **I am repeating uplifting thoughts.**

My Empowering Affirmation:
I am _____

Guided Affirmation: **I am giving my best and providing value to others.**

My Empowering Affirmation:
I am _____

Guided Affirmation: **I am serene.**

My Empowering Affirmation:
I am _____

Guided Affirmation: **I am giving my best and providing value to others.**

My Empowering Affirmation:
I am _____

Guided Affirmation: **I am confident and fierce.**

My Empowering Affirmation:
I am _____

Guided Affirmation: **I am giving my best and providing value to others.**

My Empowering Affirmation:
I am _____

Guided Affirmation: **I am producing positive results in all areas of my life.**

My Empowering Affirmation:
I am _____

Guided Affirmation: **I am giving my best and providing value to others.**

My Empowering Affirmation:
I am _____

Guided Affirmation: **I am releasing resentment and feeling joy.**

My Empowering Affirmation:
I am _____

Guided Affirmation: **I am giving my best and providing value to others.**

My Empowering Affirmation:
I am _____

Guided Affirmation: **I am positive and affirm constructive thoughts.**

My Empowering Affirmation:
I am _____

Guided Affirmation: **I am giving my best and providing value to others.**

My Empowering Affirmation:
I am _____

Guided Affirmation: **I am talented.**

My Empowering Affirmation:
I am _____

Guided Affirmation: **I am giving my best and providing value to others.**

My Empowering Affirmation:
I am _____

Guided Affirmation: **I am declaring and creating amazing experiences.**

My Empowering Affirmation:
I am _____

Guided Affirmation: **I am giving my best and providing value to others.**

My Empowering Affirmation:
I am _____

Guided Affirmation: **I am confident and courageous.**

My Empowering Affirmation:
I am _____

Guided Affirmation: **I am giving my best and providing value to others.**

My Empowering Affirmation:
I am _____

Guided Affirmation: **I am living my life fully guided by my values.**

My Empowering Affirmation:
I am _____

Guided Affirmation: **I am giving my best and providing value to others.**

My Empowering Affirmation:
I am _____

Guided Affirmation: **I am releasing worry and feeling peace.**

My Empowering Affirmation:
I am _____

Guided Affirmation: **I am giving my best and providing value to others.**

My Empowering Affirmation:
I am _____

Guided Affirmation: **I am taking care of my mental and emotional needs.**

My Empowering Affirmation:
I am _____

Guided Affirmation: **I am giving my best and providing value to others.**

My Empowering Affirmation:
I am _____

Guided Affirmation: **I am creative.**

My Empowering Affirmation:
I am _____

Guided Affirmation: **I am giving my best and providing value to others.**

My Empowering Affirmation:
I am _____

Guided Affirmation: **I am boldly making right choices for me.**

My Empowering Affirmation:
I am _____

Guided Affirmation: **I am giving my best and providing value to others.**

My Empowering Affirmation:
I am _____

Guided Affirmation: **I am secure in who I am.**

My Empowering Affirmation:
I am _____

Guided Affirmation: **I am giving my best and providing value to others.**

My Empowering Affirmation:
I am _____

Guided Affirmation: **I am giving myself unconditional love.**

My Empowering Affirmation:
I am _____

Guided Affirmation: **I am giving my best and providing value to others.**

My Empowering Affirmation:
I am _____

Guided Affirmation: **I am releasing anger and feeling calm.**

My Empowering Affirmation:
I am _____

Guided Affirmation: **I am giving my best and providing value to others.**

My Empowering Affirmation:
I am _____

Guided Affirmation: **I am celebrating my positive actions.**

My Empowering Affirmation:
I am _____

Guided Affirmation: **I am giving my best and providing value to others.**

My Empowering Affirmation:
I am _____

Guided Affirmation: **I am abundance.**

My Empowering Affirmation:

I am _____

Guided Affirmation: **I am giving my best and providing value to others.**

My Empowering Affirmation:
I am _____

Guided Affirmation: **I am continuously defining and creating my ideal life.**

My Empowering Affirmation:
I am _____

Guided Affirmation: **I am giving my best and providing value to others.**

My Empowering Affirmation:
I am _____

Guided Affirmation: **I am worthy of love and acceptance.**

My Empowering Affirmation:
I am _____

Guided Affirmation: **I am giving my best and providing value to others.**

My Empowering Affirmation:
I am _____

Guided Affirmation: **I am committed to live by who I am and what I believe.**

My Empowering Affirmation:
I am _____

Guided Affirmation: **I am giving my best and providing value to others.**

My Empowering Affirmation:
I am _____

Guided Affirmation: **I am releasing hatred and feeling love.**

My Empowering Affirmation:
I am _____

Guided Affirmation: **I am giving my best and providing value to others.**

My Empowering Affirmation:
I am _____

Guided Affirmation: **I am creating positive experiences.**

My Empowering Affirmation:
I am _____

Guided Affirmation: **I am giving my best and providing value to others.**

My Empowering Affirmation:
I am _____

Guided Affirmation: **I am accepting change with ease.**

My Empowering Affirmation:
I am _____

Guided Affirmation: **I am giving my best and providing value to others.**

My Empowering Affirmation:
I am _____

Guided Affirmation: **I am declaring, believing and achieving my goals.**

My Empowering Affirmation:
I am _____

Guided Affirmation: **I am giving my best and providing value to others.**

My Empowering Affirmation:
I am _____

Guided Affirmation: **I am deeply in love with myself.**

My Empowering Affirmation:
I am _____

Guided Affirmation: **I am giving my best and providing value to others.**

My Empowering Affirmation:
I am _____

Guided Affirmation: **I am valuable.**

My Empowering Affirmation:
I am _____

Guided Affirmation: **I am giving my best and providing value to others.**

My Empowering Affirmation:
I am _____

Guided Affirmation: **I am present and living in the moment.**

My Empowering Affirmation:
I am _____

Guided Affirmation: **I am giving my best and providing value to others.**

My Empowering Affirmation:
I am _____

Guided Affirmation: **I am peaceful.**

My Empowering Affirmation:
I am _____

Guided Affirmation: **I am giving my best and providing value to others.**

My Empowering Affirmation:
I am _____

Guided Affirmation: **I am driven in all areas of my life.**

My Empowering Affirmation:
I am _____

Guided Affirmation: **I am giving my best and providing value to others.**

My Empowering Affirmation:
I am _____

Guided Affirmation: **I am repeating positive thoughts, and feeling happy.**

My Empowering Affirmation:
I am _____

Guided Affirmation: **I am giving my best and providing value to others.**

My Empowering Affirmation:
I am _____

Guided Affirmation: **I am being myself, and fully secure in who I am.**

My Empowering Affirmation:
I am _____

Guided Affirmation: **I am giving my best and providing value to others.**

My Empowering Affirmation:
I am _____

Guided Affirmation: **I am developing my abilities and talents.**

My Empowering Affirmation:
I am _____

Guided Affirmation: **I am giving my best and providing value to others.**

My Empowering Affirmation:
I am _____

Guided Affirmation: **I am limitless.**

My Empowering Affirmation:
I am _____

Guided Affirmation: **I am giving my best and providing value to others.**

My Empowering Affirmation:
I am _____

Guided Affirmation: **I am loveable.**

My Empowering Affirmation:
I am _____

Guided Affirmation: **I am giving my best and providing value to others.**

My Empowering Affirmation:
I am _____

Guided Affirmation: **I am motivated to change for my personal growth.**

My Empowering Affirmation:
I am _____

Guided Affirmation: **I am giving my best and providing value to others.**

My Empowering Affirmation:
I am _____

Guided Affirmation: **I am connected with my goodness within.**

My Empowering Affirmation:
I am _____

Guided Affirmation: **I am giving my best and providing value to others.**

My Empowering Affirmation:
I am _____

Guided Affirmation: **I am integrity.**

My Empowering Affirmation:
I am _____

Guided Affirmation: **I am giving my best and providing value to others.**

My Empowering Affirmation:
I am _____

Guided Affirmation: **I am focusing my mind on thoughts that serve me well.**

My Empowering Affirmation:
I am _____

Guided Affirmation: **I am giving my best and providing value to others.**

My Empowering Affirmation:
I am _____

Guided Affirmation: **I am absorbing constructive knowledge, and growing.**

My Empowering Affirmation:
I am _____

Guided Affirmation: **I am giving my best and providing value to others.**

My Empowering Affirmation:
I am _____

Guided Affirmation: **I am radiating my positive personal power.**

My Empowering Affirmation:
I am _____

Guided Affirmation: **I am giving my best and providing value to others.**

My Empowering Affirmation:
I am _____

Guided Affirmation: **I am authentic.**

My Empowering Affirmation:
I am _____

Guided Affirmation: **I am giving my best and providing value to others.**

My Empowering Affirmation:
I am _____

Guided Affirmation: **I am powerful.**

My Empowering Affirmation:
I am _____

Guided Affirmation: **I am giving my best and providing value to others.**

My Empowering Affirmation:
I am _____

Guided Affirmation: **I am consciously evolving into my greater self.**

My Empowering Affirmation:
I am _____

Guided Affirmation: **I am giving my best and providing value to others.**

My Empowering Affirmation:
I am _____

Guided Affirmation: **I am repeating thoughts that are uplifting and loving.**

My Empowering Affirmation:
I am _____

Guided Affirmation: **I am giving my best and providing value to others.**

My Empowering Affirmation:
I am _____

Guided Affirmation: **I am thriving mentally and emotionally.**

My Empowering Affirmation:
I am _____

Guided Affirmation: **I am giving my best and providing value to others.**

My Empowering Affirmation:
I am _____

Guided Affirmation: **I am charged with positive energy.**

My Empowering Affirmation:
I am _____

Guided Affirmation: **I am giving my best and providing value to others.**

My Empowering Affirmation:
I am _____

Guided Affirmation: **I am awesome.**

My Empowering Affirmation:
I am _____

Guided Affirmation: **I am giving my best and providing value to others.**

My Empowering Affirmation:
I am _____

Guided Affirmation: **I am empowered.**

My Empowering Affirmation:
I am _____

Guided Affirmation: **I am giving my best and providing value to others.**

My Empowering Affirmation:
I am _____

Guided Affirmation: **I am grateful for who I am.**

My Empowering Affirmation:

I am _____

Guided Affirmation: **I am giving my best and providing value to others.**

List of guided affirmations:

- I am focusing my mind on positive thoughts and images.
- I am worthy.
- I am creating life goals that are inspiring and realistic.
- I am joyful.
- I am composed, even during moments of trouble.
- I am deserving.
- I am goal-oriented and taking action.
- I am calm and feeling peaceful.
- I am releasing fear and feeling bold.
- I am thinking clearly and optimistically.
- I am unstoppable.
- I am focused, and actively creating my dreams.
- I am overcoming challenges.
- I am deserving of feeling joy and peace.
- I am confident and powerful.
- I am imaginative.
- I am releasing disappointment and feeling grateful.
- I am confidently repeating powerful thoughts.
- I am grateful.
- I am designing and living a joyful life.
- I am successfully managing my problems.
- I am good enough.
- I am intelligent and gifted.
- I am self-compassionate.
- I am releasing doubt and feeling confident.
- I am repeating positive and affirming thoughts.
- I am passionate.
- I am creating a happy and fulfilling life.
- I am focused and disciplined.
- I am living a purposeful life.

List of guided affirmations:

- I am releasing sorrow and feeling hopeful.
- I am nurturing an abundance mindset.
- I am dependable.
- I am creating my happiness.
- I am manifesting my dreams.
- I am worthy of all good things that come my way.
- I am unique and magnificent.
- I am intentional in all areas of my life.
- I am releasing envy and feeling love.
- I am repeating uplifting thoughts.
- I am serene.
- I am confident and fierce.
- I am producing positive results in all areas of my life.
- I am releasing resentment and feeling joy.
- I am positive and affirm constructive thoughts.
- I am talented.
- I am declaring and creating amazing experiences.
- I am confident and courageous.
- I am living my life fully guided by my values.
- I am releasing worry and feeling peace.
- I am taking care of my mental and emotional needs.
- I am creative.
- I am boldly making right choices for me.
- I am secure in who I am.
- I am giving myself unconditional love.
- I am releasing anger and feeling calm.
- I am celebrating my positive actions.
- I am abundance.
- I am continuously defining and creating my ideal life.
- I am worthy of love and acceptance.

List of guided affirmations:

♦ I am committed to live by who I am and what I believe.

♦ I am releasing hatred and feeling love.

♦ I am creating positive experiences.

♦ I am accepting change with ease.

♦ I am declaring, believing and achieving my goals.

♦ I am deeply in love with myself.

♦ I am valuable.

♦ I am present and living in the moment.

♦ I am peaceful.

♦ I am driven in all areas of my life.

♦ I am repeating positive thoughts, and feeling happy.

♦ I am being myself, and fully secure in who I am.

♦ I am developing my abilities and talents.

♦ I am limitless.

♦ I am loveable.

♦ I am motivated to change for my personal growth.

♦ I am connected with my goodness within.

♦ I am integrity.

♦ I am focusing my mind on thoughts that serve me well.

♦ I am absorbing constructive knowledge, and growing.

♦ I am radiating my positive personal power.

♦ I am authentic.

♦ I am powerful.

♦ I am consciously evolving into my greater self.

♦ I am repeating thoughts that are uplifting and loving.

♦ I am thriving mentally and emotionally.

♦ I am charged with positive energy.

♦ I am awesome.

♦ I am empowered.

♦ I am grateful for who I am.

♦ I am giving my best and providing value to others.

Hella

I think your are so handsome and cute
you are like my sweet dreams in every
moments and I'm wishing to be with you
so I can look into your eyes and hold
your hands or you probably hug me kiss
me however you want on cheeks or
forehead which is my favorite I can
say I love you and you probably
really love me too or just stay
and please don't leave they say
boys only want love if it's torture
I will be so nice to you I will never
bother you I promise but it's probably
like I love the players and you love
the game anyway I'm your queen
and if I get a blank space I will write
your name. you are my baby so
stay close and falling in love
so baby baby and let's make it
perfect! love you to the moon
and back baby

Your Girlfriend ♡

:")